HIDDEN WORLDS
THE INCAS
and MACHU PICCHU

by Philip Steele

A ZOË BOOK

A ZOË BOOK

© 1993 Zoë Books Limited

Devised and produced by
Zoë Books Limited
15 Worthy Lane
Winchester
Hampshire SO23 7AB
England

First published in Great Britain in 1993 by
Zoë Books Limited
15 Worthy Lane
Winchester
Hampshire SO23 7AB

A record of the CIP data is available from the British
Library.

ISBN 1 874488 14 2

Printed in Italy by Grafedit SpA
Design: Jan Sterling, Sterling Associates
Picture research: Suzanne Williams
Maps: Gecko Limited
Production: Grahame Griffiths

Photographic acknowledgements
The publishers wish to acknowledge, with thanks, the
following photographic sources:

The Hutchison Library: 12/Eric Lawrie; Marion and
Tony Morrison, South American Pictures: title page,
5, 6, 10, 14, 15t & b, 16t & b, 17t & b, 18, 19t & b,
20t & b, 21, 22t & b, 23, 24t & b, 25b, 26t & b, 27,
28t & b; Courtesy of the National Geographic
Society, photographs taken by Hiram Bingham or
under his direction and reproduced in the *National
Geographic Magazine*, April 1913: 7t & b, 8t & b, 9,
11b; © Yale University, Peabody Museum of Natural
History/Syndication International: 25t; Zefa:
cover/Kurt Goebel, 11t/Hed Weisner, 29/J
Schörken

Contents

Children of the Sun   4

In search of the lost city   6

Return to Machu Picchu   8

Archaeologists at work   10

The city revealed   12

Rulers and ruled   14

Priests and warriors   16

Science – and magic   18

Builders and engineers   20

The harvest and the hunt   22

Bronze, gold and feathers   24

Everyday life   26

Past, present and future   28

Glossary   30

Index   32

Children of the Sun

Peru is a country in South America, beside the waters of the Pacific Ocean. Near its coast there are low-lying deserts, but inland there are the high, snowy peaks of the Andes Mountains. Beyond these mountains are dense tropical forests and a maze of rivers which drain into the mighty Amazon River.

Between about 3000 and 500 years ago, several **civilizations** grew up in ancient Peru. The greatest was that of the Incas.

▶ The power of the Incas was at its greatest between the years 1493 and 1525. The **empire** stretched for almost 3500 kilometres along the Pacific coastline and for about 320 km inland. Its power extended into the lands now known as Colombia, Ecuador, Chile, Bolivia and Argentina. A network of roads linked the main towns of the empire.

The Inca people settled in the Cuzco region, high in the Andes, about 900 years ago. In AD 1438 the Inca ruler, Pachacuti Inca Yupanqui, built up a powerful state around Cuzco. His son conquered the powerful Chimú people so that vast areas of land became part of an Inca empire.

Peru was soon torn apart by **civil war**. In 1532 the ruler Huascar was overthrown by his brother Atahualpa. More trouble was to come. Stories of the Inca empire and its fabulous wealth had spread to distant Europe. These rumours said that the Inca rulers wore gold and claimed descent from the Sun itself.

No sooner had Atahualpa become emperor than a small force of Spanish soldiers arrived in Peru, led by Francisco Pizarro. They were greedy for gold and wanted to conquer the country for themselves.

Pizarro captured Atahualpa by treachery and demanded a high **ransom** for him. Although the Incas paid the Spanish soldiers a fortune, the Spaniards put the Inca ruler to a cruel death.

Many Incas fought bravely against the Spanish until 1572, but the Europeans were in South America to stay. The greatest empire of ancient Peru was to be the last.

◀ The Spanish entered the town of Cajamarca in November 1532. They were received by Atahualpa. When he was shown the Bible, he cast it aside. Many Incas believed that the Spanish had been sent by the Sun god. In fact they had to come to kill. The Spanish massacred 7000 Inca warriors at Cajamarca and murdered Atahualpa the following summer.

In search of the lost city

Spanish rule was harsh. The peoples of the former Inca empire worked on the land and in the mines. They became very poor, while the Europeans became richer and richer.

The Inca temples were stripped of their gold and destroyed. Graves were broken open and any precious objects they contained were stolen and sold. The treasures of a great civilization were being destroyed or lost. The forest began to grow back over many Inca towns. Creepers grew over the ruined stone walls.

It was not until the 1800s that people around the world began to realise that such treasures should be preserved. Ancient sites were dug up, or **excavated**, and their remains were studied scientifically. A new interest grew up in **archaeology**.

▼ Machu Picchu lies on a ridge 610 metres above the Urubamba River. Rising in the Andes, the Urubamba flows through steep gorges for 720 km before it joins with the Apurímac to form the great Ucayali River.

The first expedition

In 1911, Dr Hiram Bingham, an American archaeologist, came to Peru from Yale University. Bingham was fascinated by the lost world of the Incas. He had read how the Incas had made a final stand against the Spanish at a place called Vilcabamba. Perhaps he could find the ruins of their last stronghold. Bingham travelled to Cuzco, the old Inca capital.

From Cuzco, he followed a mule track to a remote area 100 km to the north. On the sixth day he came to a small plantation called Mandorpampa. Here, an old man offered to guide the American to some hidden ruins.

A dangerous-looking bridge of logs took them across the rushing white waters of the Urubamba River. They began to climb a steep path through the forest. The twin mountains of Machu Picchu and Huayna Picchu towered above them, and soon the river lay far below.

Hiram Bingham could see traces of terraced fields, or **andenes**. Suddenly, he could scarcely believe his eyes. Ahead of the guide a maze of ruined walls appeared, covered in roots and plants. Here, amidst the high peaks of the Andes, was surely one of the most breathtaking sites in all the Americas!

▲ In the 1900s the countryside around Machu Picchu was still very wild. This mule track on the banks of the Urubamba River had only just been opened up. It led Dr Hiram Bingham to a vanished world.

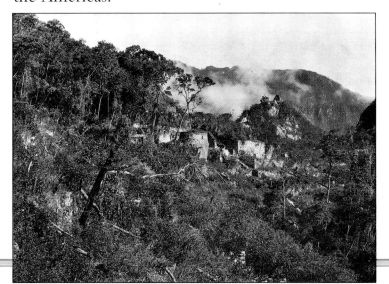

◄ Dr Hiram Bingham took this photograph of Machu Picchu after clearing the undergrowth for ten days. The impressive ruins were beginning to emerge from the jungle.

Return to Machu Picchu

Hiram Bingham returned to the United States full of enthusiasm. He was determined to map and excavate this lost city of the Incas. He planned a second expedition, with the support of Yale University and the *National Geographic Magazine*.

Bingham's first job was to find a team of experts. He needed other archaeologists who could help him. He also needed a geographer to help to prepare maps of the area. Bingham knew that if he found human remains, the bones would help him to date the site and to find out how it had been used by the Incas. So he recruited a bone specialist, an **osteologist**, for the expedition.

The expedition assembled in Peru and on 12 July 1912, Kenneth Heald, Bingham's assistant, set out from Cuzco. His job was to prepare a route for the others. Heald built a new bridge across the Urubamba River, to the east of the Machu Picchu site. He then cut a trail through thickets of bamboo. In many places he had to clear away the dense undergrowth by burning it.

At last the way was open. Bingham set out, his porters carrying the boxes of precious supplies. They crossed the Urubamba and toiled up to the ridge, where they set up camp.

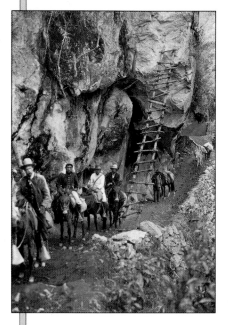

▲ All the expedition's heavy equipment had to be carried along the trail by mules or by people. In 1912, the archaeologists could not use helicopters or four-wheel drive vehicles, as they might do today.

▶ Kenneth Heald was the expedition's pioneer. He went ahead of the main party and lashed together this bridge over the rapids of the Urubamba River.

Bingham's first job was to **survey** the site. He needed to know more about the lie of the land and to map the boundaries of the site. The settlement had been built at 2743 metres above sea level, and covered about 40 hectares.

Kenneth Heald was sent to climb the peak of Huayna Picchu. Scrambling up the mountain-side, he nearly plunged to his death. Luckily he survived and reached the top on a second attempt. There was only a small ruined building there, perhaps an Inca look-out post. It seemed that the main site was on the lower ridge, or **saddle**, between the two peaks, Huayna and Machu Picchu.

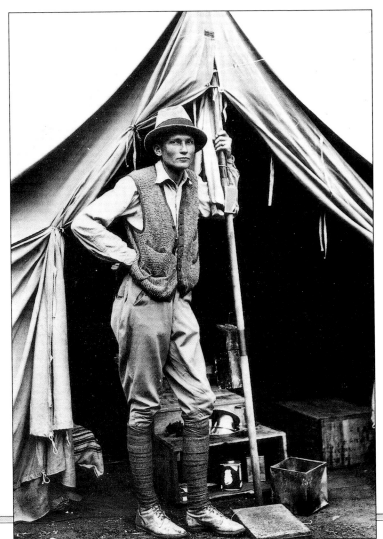

◀ Dr Hiram Bingham in the expedition's camp at Machu Picchu. He was sure that the site had played an important part in Inca history.

Archaeologists at work

The hard work of the archaeologists now began. As they hacked the undergrowth away, it became clear that the ancient stonework had survived very well. Only where large trees had rooted in the walls were there problems. There were fears that removing the tree roots might break up the **masonry**.

Buildings were mapped and measured. Some houses had been so cleverly constructed that Hiram Bingham called them the 'Ingenuity' group. The stones fitted together so well that they did not need **mortar** to hold them in place.

Excavations began in two promising places, the Principal Temple and the Temple of the Three Windows. Trenches were dug to depths of up to three metres. To Bingham's

▼ The Temple of the Three Windows was examined by Hiram Bingham during his first expedition. The 'windows' were three large openings in a massive stone wall. Bingham recalled an ancient Inca legend. It told how the Incas of Cuzco had first come from a place called *Tampu Tocco*, which means 'tavern of the windows'. Could this have been the same place?

disappointment, nothing was found at these sites. He had hoped to find objects, or **artefacts**, made by the Incas.

Inca burials

Over 100 burial sites were discovered, mostly in natural caves on the slopes beneath the city. A few were in hollowed-out chambers in the city itself. One site was 300 metres above the city, beneath a rock. Each site was carefully photographed, drawn and measured.

The skeletons of the Incas had been buried as if they were sitting with their knees drawn up. Artefacts were buried with them. There were pots, tweezers, shawl pins and a knife and mirror made of bronze. There were traces of wool and vegetable fibre, all that remained of the people's clothing.

The archaeologists found a total of 173 skeletons. Hiram Bingham was puzzled, because 150 of these were females, who seemed to have been wealthy. An old legend in Peru said that the High Priestess and the holy women, or *mamacuna*, had fled from Cuzco during the Spanish invasion. Might they have come here, to Machu Picchu?

▲ This cave at Machu Picchu has a triangular entrance. Its steps are cut out of solid rock. The Incas used caves as burial places.

◀ This photograph was taken by Hiram Bingham. A team of local workers is excavating the site of the main temple in Machu Picchu.

The city revealed

The archaeologists at Machu Picchu uncovered a mountain stronghold built from blocks of a hard, white rock called **granite**. Perched on the mountain ridge, the city could be approached from one side only. It was defended by a double wall and a dry ditch, or moat. The wooden city gates were unlocked to allow people in and out. On the outskirts of the city the soldiers lived in **barracks**.

The city was built on rising ground, so the buildings were at various heights. Some were built into solid rock, but most were on terraces made of stone blocks. The steep streets included 100 stone stairways, each with up to 100 steps. Water was supplied by the mountain springs of Machu Picchu, 1.5 km away. The water was carried to the city along an **aqueduct** and was channelled to the houses, fountains and gardens.

At the centre of the city was the Great Plaza. This was where public announcements were made.

▼ Thanks to the archaeologists, the outlines of Machu Picchu may now be clearly seen. The sun breaks through the clouds to show the outlines of the ancient buildings.

The Incas believed that the Sun was the most important of all the gods. The holiest part of the city was probably the Sun Stone, the *Intihuatana*. Temples were built on high ground, and nearby were the palaces of the nobles.

In the outer parts of Machu Picchu were the houses of farmers, labourers and craft workers. Here there were public storehouses for food and other supplies.

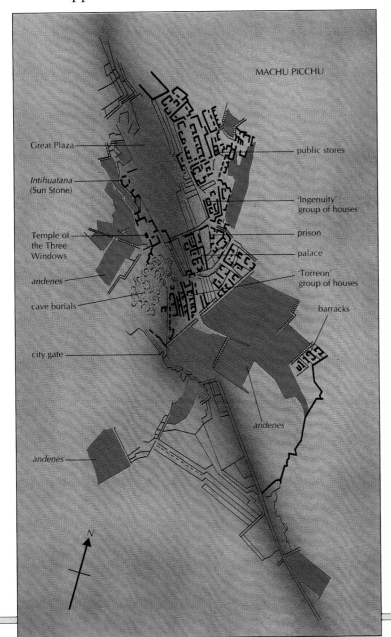

MACHU PICCHU

Great Plaza

Intihuatana (Sun Stone)

Temple of the Three Windows

andenes

cave burials

city gate

andenes

public stores

'Ingenuity' group of houses

prison

palace

'Torreon' group of houses

barracks

andenes

N

◀ About 1000 people lived in Machu Picchu. It was very much smaller than Cuzco. It was built about 500 years ago, when Inca power was at its height.

Rulers and ruled

The remains at Machu Picchu have helped historians to piece together the details of how the Incas lived from day to day. As the buildings were cleared of creepers and bushes, it became obvious that the houses of the nobles were separated from the more humble dwellings. Inca society was divided into strict **social classes**. The city was also divided into groups of families or **clan** areas. The members of each clan, or *ayllu*, were usually descended from the same ancestor.

▶ Archaeology can tell us how people lived in ancient times. In Machu Picchu the houses of the nobles were at the centre of the town, away from the houses of the ordinary people.

At the top of the social order was the emperor or *Sapa Inca*. In the later period of Inca power, the emperor married one of his own sisters. She became the empress, or *Coya*. The emperor also had hundreds of less important wives, who were chosen from the most beautiful girls in the empire.

The many children born to the emperor became nobles. The men worked as regional governors, priests, judges and army officers. The chiefs of the tribes which were conquered by the Incas could also keep their high rank, if they promised to be loyal to the emperor and to worship the Sun.

For the lower classes, everyday life was made up of hard work. Crops and other products had to be given to the public stores. In Machu Picchu the storehouses were sited in the north of the city. Goods were then handed out according to need, and officials made sure that the elderly and the infirm were given a share of food and clothing.

Running the empire

The government was very efficient. The Inca's wishes were carried out by the four officers or **prefects** of the Supreme Council. Each prefect represented one quarter of the empire. The Inca name for Peru was *Tahuantinsuyu*, or 'the four quarters' (north, south, east and west).

Money was not used in ancient Peru, so **taxes** were paid in the form of crops, labour or military service. Nobles and officials did not have to pay taxes. The number of people in each town was counted regularly. The Incas used a system of counting off in groups of ten.

Machu Picchu had a prison to the southwest of the Great Plaza. Laws were strict and punishments were severe.

▼ The *Sapa Inca* ruled from Cuzco, but he travelled around the empire with the *Coya*. This picture was drawn in the 1600s by Guaman Poma de Alaya. It shows the famous emperor Topa Inca Yupanqui, who ruled from 1471 to 1493.

▼ Workers carry sacks of grain into the public storehouse. Ordinary people were not allowed to travel around the empire. They had to stay at home and work in the fields. Some were sent to live in lands that had been conquered by the Inca armies.

Priests and warriors

► The Sun Stone, or *Intihuatana*, casts a shadow at Machu Picchu. It recorded the movement of the Sun across the sky. The Incas worshipped both the Sun and the Moon, and their children – the stars.

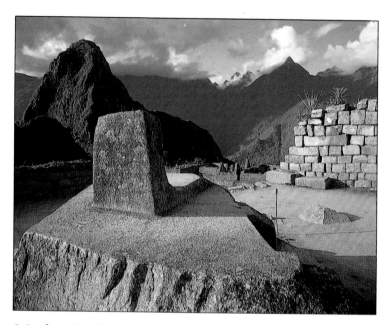

Machu Picchu had many fine temples. There were also places where people were killed as an offering, or sacrifice to the gods and goddesses. To the east of the Great Plaza, Hiram Bingham discovered the great rock of the Sun Stone, or *Intihuatana*.

The Incas believed that a god called Viracocha was the maker or **creator** of the world, the Sun and the Moon. On Earth, the Inca emperor represented the Sun god, *Inti*. The empress represented the Moon goddess, *Mama-quilla*. The thunder god, *Illapa*, was the messenger of the Sun. The harvest was looked after by the earth mother, *Pacha-mama*, and on the coast, fishing people worshipped *Mama-cocha*, the sea goddess.

▲ This gold mask is made in the shape of the Sun, the god of the *Sapa Inca*. It was treasure such as this which attracted the Spanish soldiers to Peru.

The Incas worshipped at temples and also at local holy places, or shrines, called *huacas*. Holy places and objects included stones, springs, tombs and caves. There were men and women priests. Some girls were chosen to become *mamacuna* or the unmarried *acllas*. They vowed to live a religious life and to serve in the temples.

The most important worship was of the Sun god, and this fact helped to make the emperor all-powerful. He was not only the religious head of his people, but the commander-in-chief of the Inca armies.

Armies of the Sun

Army officers were trained at an early age. The serving soldiers were fed from storehouses which were set up in every corner of the empire. Troops were well-drilled, and fought with spears, swords and axes made of bone, stone, hardened wood or copper. They also had bows and arrows, clubs and maces, slings, and *bolas* (three stones tied to long strings). Shields and helmets were made of wood, and armour was made of thick pads of cotton.

Different ranks in the army wore various badges and head-dresses. Armies went into battle with colourful standards and played drums and flutes, sometimes made from the skin and bones of their enemies. However, the lives of defeated enemy soldiers were often spared.

▲ Nobles from Machu Picchu may have travelled to Cuzco for *Inti Raymi*, the great festival of the Sun. There would be dancing, feasting and sacrifices to the Sun god.

◀ Today, people in Cuzco keep alive the great festival of the Sun, or *Inti Raymi*. In Inca times nobles from Machu Picchu probably travelled to Cuzco each year in order to feast, dance and make sacrifices to the Sun god.

Science – and magic

▲ The plant with the yellow flower is called calceolaria. It was used in a medicine which cured infections. In Inca times, a person who was skilled at curing sick people was called a *hampi camayoc*. As in Europe during this time, medicine was a mixture of genuine cures and superstitions.

The Incas were skilled doctors and surgeons. They made healing or pain-killing drugs such as **quinine**, tobacco and **coca** from herbs and the bark of trees or from the leaves of forest plants. They were also able to operate on people's skulls. The Incas believed that magic was the cause of most sickness. Treatments often included religious ceremonies or **rituals**, which were intended to drive out evil spirits.

The Incas had little resistance to common European illnesses, such as measles. After the Spanish invasion, many Inca people became ill and died.

The Sun, Moon and stars played an important part in the religious beliefs of the Incas. They studied how the stars and planets moved around, which is called **astronomy**. They also worked out a calendar, to help to decide when to plant their crops.

Arithmetic was based on a **decimal system**. Counting frames were divided into twenty sections, each containing seeds or pebbles. The cleverest way of counting was by using a system of knotted cords called *quipus*.

Education

The ordinary people of Machu Picchu learned the skills of farming, weaving or building from their parents. The emperors claimed that too much education was bad for ordinary working people.

Girls chosen to serve in the temples, as *mamacuna* or *acllas*, were educated in special schools or **convents**. The sons of nobles were sent to school in Cuzco, where they studied religion, poetry, *quipu*, arithmetic, history and Quechua, which was the main language of the Inca empire.

▲ The *quipu* was made up of a cord tied with strings. The knots tied in the strings formed a code.

◀ People were trained to use the *quipu* for taking the **census** or for keeping accounts. *Quipus* were also used to help people to remember long lists of historical events, or religious rituals. At the bottom of the picture on the left is a counting frame.

19

Builders and engineers

The archaeologists discovered that the granite walls of Machu Picchu were built by experts. The Incas did not use mortar to cement the blocks together, but today the edges still fit together so closely that a knife blade cannot be pushed in between. The walls lock together so well that even if they are shaken by an earthquake they often fall back into position.

The people who planned the buildings, the **architects**, were nobles. They used small working models made of stone. The labourers were ordinary people, who worked as a means of paying their taxes. They cut the blocks of stone from the quarries, and shaped them, smoothing down the surface with sand and water. The stones were moved by rolling them along on logs. They were raised with ramps and bronze **crowbars**.

Most buildings had only one level, or **storey**. Buildings with two storeys were linked by rope

▲ The blocks of granite at Machu Picchu were shaped until they fitted together exactly. Roof beams were tied to the stone pegs.

▶ Stone steps lead past a house at Machu Picchu. The building has been thatched with *ichu* grass to show how it would have looked 500 years ago.

◀ A public official keeps watch over the rope bridge. The Incas built rope bridges across river valleys and mountain gorges. They were up to 60 metres long. Small bridges were made of stone and many survive today.

ladders or by stepping stones set in the outer wall. At Machu Picchu, the roofs sloped steeply, so that the water would run off during heavy rain storms.

Roads and bridges

At the time of the Spanish invasion of Peru, roads in Europe were little more than muddy tracks. However, in the Inca empire the roads were built by experts. There were more than 16 000 kilometres of road, and much of it was paved. Stone or rope bridges were built across rivers and gorges. Stone markers recorded the distance in *topos*, which were units of about 10 kilometres. The Incas built rest houses and public stores by the roadside. There were huts for officials and for the relay runners who carried messages to and from the emperor.

Nobles were carried around in hand-held carriages without wheels, called **litters**. Surprisingly, the Incas did not know how to make wheels. Goods were carried by people or on the backs of **llamas**, the animals which are still used in the Andes today.

The harvest and the hunt

▶ The terraced fields were filled with good soil. Their walls prevented the precious earth from being washed away by the rain or blown off the mountain-side by the wind.

▼ *Quinoa* ripens in the Peruvian Andes. This was grown as a food crop by Inca farmers.

The stone walls of the terraced fields, the *andenes*, at Machu Picchu, have survived for more than 400 years. They show clearly how much the Incas depended on farming.

The most important crops in the mountains were potatoes, a root crop called *oca* and a grain called *quinoa*. In lowland regions and in the warmer mountain valleys, maize was widely grown. This was ground into flour, and made into loaves, dumplings, porridge and a kind of beer called *chicha*.

Farmers broke up the soil with digging sticks called *tacllas* and weeded with hoes made of bronze. Llama dung and sewage were used as manure. Fishmeal and seabird droppings, called *guano*, were sometimes brought to the fields from the coast. This helped to fertilize the land. The Incas were skilled at building channels to carry water over their farmland, to **irrigate** the crops.

Some land was said to 'belong to the gods'. Other land belonged to the emperor. These fields had to be sown and harvested before the people could work on the land which was for their own use.

Little meat was eaten in Machu Picchu. The farmers and their families raised and ate guinea pigs. The nobles fed upon fish and birds and on tropical fruits such as bananas, which were transported around the empire by road. Herds of llamas were grazed on mountain pastures. They were sometimes eaten, but were mostly kept for their wool or for transporting goods.

Hunting

Royal officials arranged hunts at certain times, when the public were allowed to hunt with nets and *bolas*. They killed dangerous wild animals such as bears, and caught deer, rabbits, partridges and a wild llama called a *guanaco*. The meat was shared out and cut into strips. These would be dried in the sun so that they would not go bad. The meat strips were mixed with vegetables to make stews.

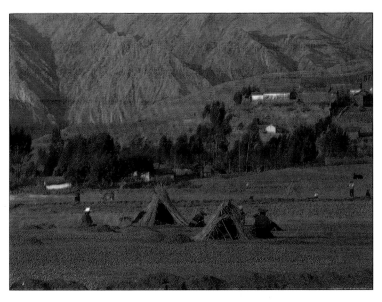

◀ Potato pickers lay out their crop to dry in the sunshine of the Peruvian Andes. The scene may have looked much the same about 500 years ago. The potato grows well in mountain regions and was first grown in the Americas.

Bronze, gold and feathers

► This fine cloak, or *poncho* was woven by Inca women. Dyes for the thread were made from plants. When the Spanish king and queen first saw Inca cloth, they marvelled at its softness and fine quality.

▼ This drinking vessel is made from wood. It is shaped like a jaguar, the fierce big cat of the South American rain-forests.

Craft workers in the Inca empire were employed by the government. They did not have to pay taxes like the labourers. The Incas had no iron, but they were experts at working with gold, silver, platinum, tin and copper. Tin and copper were melted together to make the mixture, or **alloy**, bronze.

Large amounts of tin were used for shaping or **casting** bronze. Smaller amounts were used to make the kind of bronze that was beaten into knives, axes or other tools. Small furnaces called **braziers** were discovered by archaeologists at Machu Picchu. These had been used for producing bronze and still contained traces of molten metals.

Many stone tools were also found at Machu Picchu. Some tools were used for working and polishing decorative stones, such as the green **schist** which the Incas used for making dishes and jewellery.

Llama bones were used to make all kinds of objects, from needles to spoons and flutes. Pottery was made of clay, which was often mixed with sand or shells. It was not made on a potter's wheel, but was built up in coils or, in parts of the empire, shaped by moulds. Pots were often shaped in human or animal form. Patterns were painted or scraped on the pots.

Clothes and jewellery

Few materials or **textiles** survived in the damp mountain air at Machu Picchu. In the desert regions of Peru, Inca cloth was better preserved. On the coast, cotton was grown. In the Andes, wool was taken from llamas to make coarse blankets, and from similar animals called *vicuñas* and *alpacas* to make finer cloth. All kinds of spinning and weaving tools were discovered at Machu Picchu. Tunics, cloaks, belts and headbands were woven and dyed.

Sandals were made from leather or from plaited plant fibres. Both men and women wore jewellery, and noblemen wore large gold earplugs as a badge of their rank. Feathers were used to decorate cloaks, collars and head-dresses.

▼ This little *alpaca* is made from solid silver. These animals are still bred for their fine wool.

Everyday life

▶ This is how Machu Picchu must have looked 500 years ago. Life was spent farming, cooking and weaving. Men would leave home from time to time to work in one of the public services – in the army or the mines, or on a building site.

▼ The Incas used pottery jugs to carry water from the fountains into their houses.

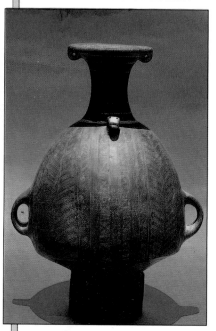

The ordinary houses at Machu Picchu were dark inside. They were draughty too, for they had no doors. Entrances were hung with a cloth. Small clay stoves provided warmth in cold weather.

Archaeologists have found no traces of wooden furniture. It may have rotted away, or perhaps the Incas did not use wood for furniture. There was a stone bench, and possessions were arranged on shelves or **niches** set in the walls, or hung on stone pegs. Food and water were kept in large pots. People slept on the floor, on mats made of reeds.

Cooking and weaving took place in the outer courtyards. Here, people could meet other members of their clan. Stone channels and fountains provided spring water for washing and bathing.

Children helped their parents with everyday chores. Men worked very hard, and women even harder, for they were expected to do the housework as well as helping in the fields.

However, there was more to life than work. The ordinary people, as well as the nobles, loved to drink, dance, play games, tell stories and make music. Musical instruments included flutes, whistles, drums, bells, rattles and **pan-pipes** made of bamboo cane. There were many family celebrations and public festivals.

Getting married

Each year a royal official called together all the unmarried men and women in town. Marriages were agreed with him. Men were usually married by the time they were 25 years old, and women by the age of twenty. Weddings were a time for gifts and feasting. A special house was prepared for each newly married couple. They did not have to pay any taxes for a year.

When a baby was born, the parents received extra land from the government. Babies were placed in a movable wooden cradle, or *quirau*. This could be placed on the ground or carried on the mother's back.

◀ All over the Inca empire people loved to play pipes, drums and other musical instruments. There was dancing on public holidays.

Past, present and future

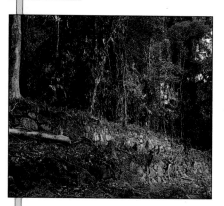

▲ Vilcabamba was discovered by American archaeologist Gene Savoy in 1964. The lost city of the Incas was sited in the Peruvian jungle. It was not high on a mountain-side like Machu Picchu.

Hiram Bingham returned to Peru in 1914, and he continued to lecture to students at Yale University until 1924. He later became a United States senator and died in 1956.

Many other archaeologists followed Bingham to Peru. Some returned to Machu Picchu. Others excavated sites in the coastal deserts and in the jungles beyond the mountains. Later archaeologists were helped by new technology and new methods of working. They could survey and photograph sites from the air. They could find out the age of cloth, bones and plant remains by a method called **radiocarbon dating**.

More and more has been revealed about the Incas and about the wonderful civilizations which came before them – the Chavin and Moche cultures and the empires of Tiahuanaco and Huari. The Spanish destroyed more than the Inca empire. They destroyed over 3000 years of Peruvian civilization.

Yet the traditions of the ancient Peruvians have not been completely forgotten. About three million Quechua people live in modern Peru. They take their name from, and speak, the

▶ A market scene in modern Peru. The Quechua people have not forgotten the empire of the Incas. For many farmers in remote mountain areas, life has changed little over the ages.

ancient Inca language. Their lives have much in common with those of their ancestors. They harvest potatoes or maize, play the pan-pipes, and weave colourful textiles. Ancient Inca ceremonies are proudly re-enacted in Cuzco, the capital of the ancient empire.

Much has changed. An international airport has now been built in Cuzco, and trains take tourists up the valley of the Urubamba river. A road twists and turns up to the ridge of Machu Picchu.

However, the site is as spectacular as ever. The fact that this was just one small part of the mighty Inca empire makes it all the more impressive. Forgetting the tourists and the cameras, it is easy to imagine life in the Andes 500 years ago. One can imagine the children playing on the steps, the officials from Cuzco busily checking the public stores, and the priests, glittering with gold, making a sacrifice to the Sun.

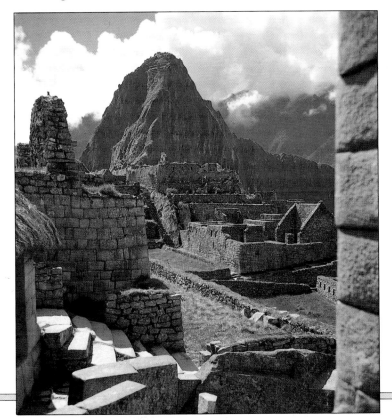

◀ Machu Picchu, high amongst the peaks of the Urubamba gorge has fascinated the world ever since its discovery over 80 years ago.

Glossary

alloy: a mixture of two or more metals.

andene: a terraced field built into the mountain side.

aqueduct: any channel built to carry water over a long distance, often raised above the ground.

archaeology: the scientific study of ancient remains.

architect: a person who designs buildings.

artefact: any object made and used by people.

astronomy: the scientific study of the night sky.

barracks: buildings where soldiers are housed.

brazier: a container of burning fuel used as a stove or furnace.

casting: pouring molten metal into a mould.

census: a count of the population.

civil war: a war which takes place between rival groups within one country.

civilization: a group of people, or society, which has made advances in government, science or the arts.

clan: a group of people descended from the same ancestors.

coca: a leaf chewed by the Incas in order to kill pain or stimulate the body. Today it is made into a dangerous drug called cocaine.

convent: a building where nuns, women who have vowed to live a religious life, live.

creator: a being or god, believed to have made the universe.

crowbar: a strong metal bar, used as a lever.

decimal system: a method of counting, based on tens.

empire: a collection of conquered or allied states, ruled over by a single government.

excavate: to dig up.

granite: a hard rock, often used for building.

irrigation: a system of watering the soil for growing crops.

litter:	a vehicle for carrying passengers. It is fitted between two hand-held shafts.
llama:	a grazing animal of South America. It is used for carrying heavy loads, and for providing wool.
masonry:	the stonework of walls or buildings.
mortar:	a mixture of lime, sand or cement, used to bind together bricks or stones.
niche:	a recess or compartment in a wall.
osteologist:	a person who studies bones.
pan-pipe:	a musical instrument made up of sections of cane, each with a different length and note.
prefect:	an official or governor.
quinine:	a valuable medicine taken from the bark of certain shrubs and trees that grow in Peru.
quipu:	a system of knots and cords, used for counting and keeping coded records.
radiocarbon dating:	measuring the rate of radioactive decay in an object, in order to date it.
ransom:	a payment demanded for the safe return of a captive.
ritual:	a religious ceremony.
saddle:	a ridge of land joining two mountain peaks.
schist:	a form of rock which contains shiny crystals.
social classes:	divisions in a society, based on wealth or power.
storey:	a floor, or level section of a building.
survey:	to take exact measurements of the land or of a site.
tax:	a sum of money or tribute paid by an individual to the government, in return for services received. The Incas did not use money, so citizens paid in produce or labour. In return, they were well cared for by the government.
textile:	cloth made by weaving.

Index

acllas 16, 19
Amazon River 4
andenes 7, 22
aqueduct 12
architecture 20
arithmetic 15, 19
army 5, 15, 17
artefacts 11
astronomy 18
battles 5, 17
Bingham, Hiram 7-11, 28
bolas 17
bridges 7, 8, 21
bronze 11, 22, 24, 25
burials 11
calendar 18
census 19
clothing 11, 15, 24, 25
cooking 26
copper 17, 24
craft workers 13, 24, 25
Cuzco 5, 7, 10, 11, 13, 17, 19, 29
desert 4, 25, 28
education 19
excavation 6, 10, 11
farming 19, 22, 26, 28
festivals 17, 27
food 13, 15, 22, 23, 26
fountains 12, 26
gods 5, 13, 16, 17, 23
gold 5, 6, 16, 24, 29
Heald, Kenneth 8, 9
houses 10, 12-14, 20, 26, 27
hunting 23
irrigation 22
jewellery 25
laws 15
llamas 21-23. 25

maize 22, 29
mamacuna 11, 16, 19
medicine 18
metalworking 24, 25
music 17, 27, 29
nobles 13-15, 17, 20, 21, 23, 26
oca 22
Pizzaro, Francisco 5
platinum 24
Plaza, Great 12, 15
potatoes 22, 23, 29
priests 5, 16, 29
pottery 11, 26
Quechua 19, 28
quinoa 22
quipu 19
radiocarbon dating 28
roads 4, 21, 23
Savoy, Gene 28
schools 19
silver 24, 25
Spanish soldiers 5, 6, 16
spinning 25
storehouses 15, 17, 21
Sun 5, 14, 15-18
Sun Stone 13, 16
taxes 15, 20, 24, 27
temples 6, 10, 11, 13, 16, 17, 19
textiles 25, 29
tin 24, 25
Ucayali River 6
Urubamba River 6-8, 29
vicuñas 25
Vilcabamba 7, 28
Viracocha 16
weapons 17
weaving 19, 25, 26, 29
wild animals 23